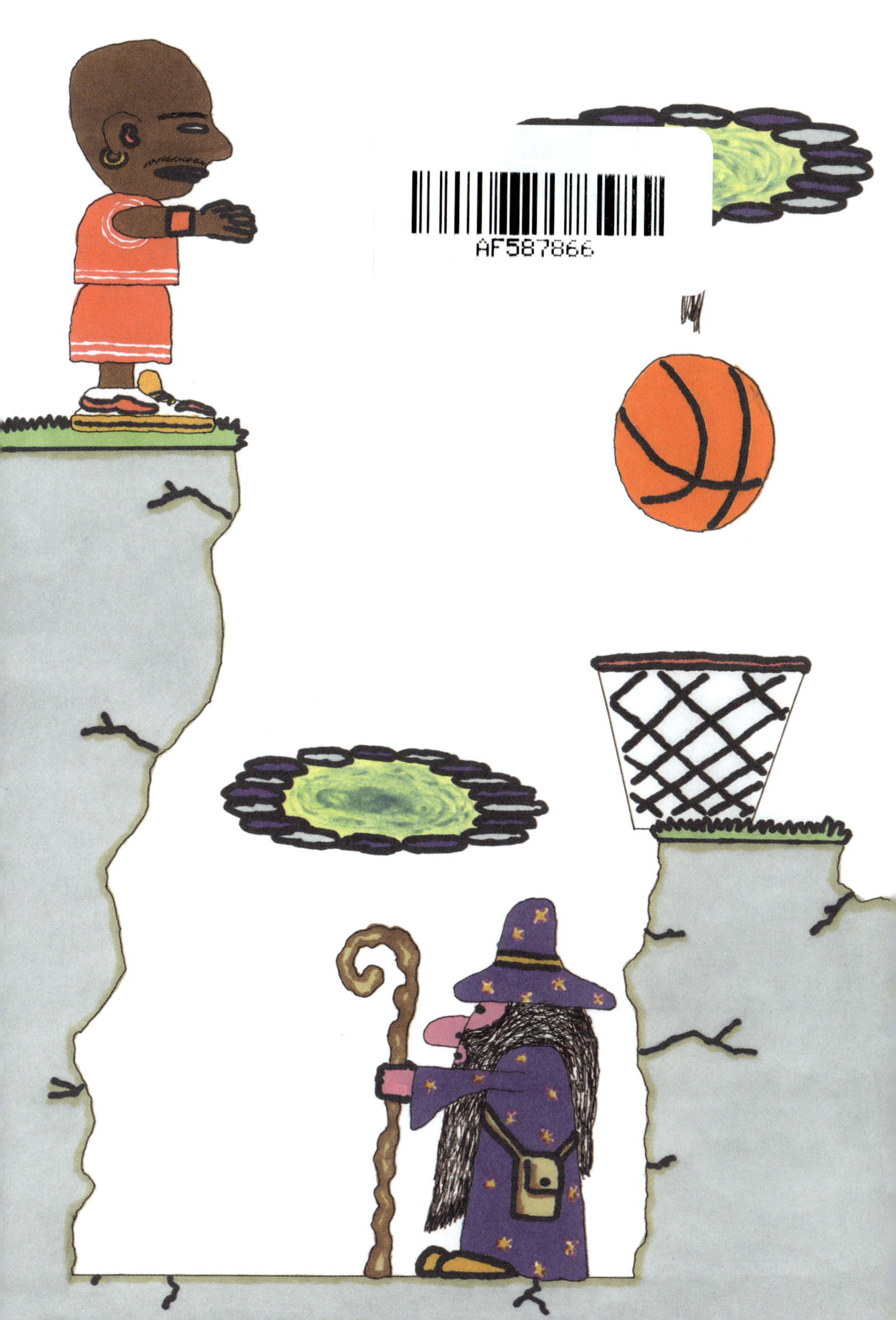

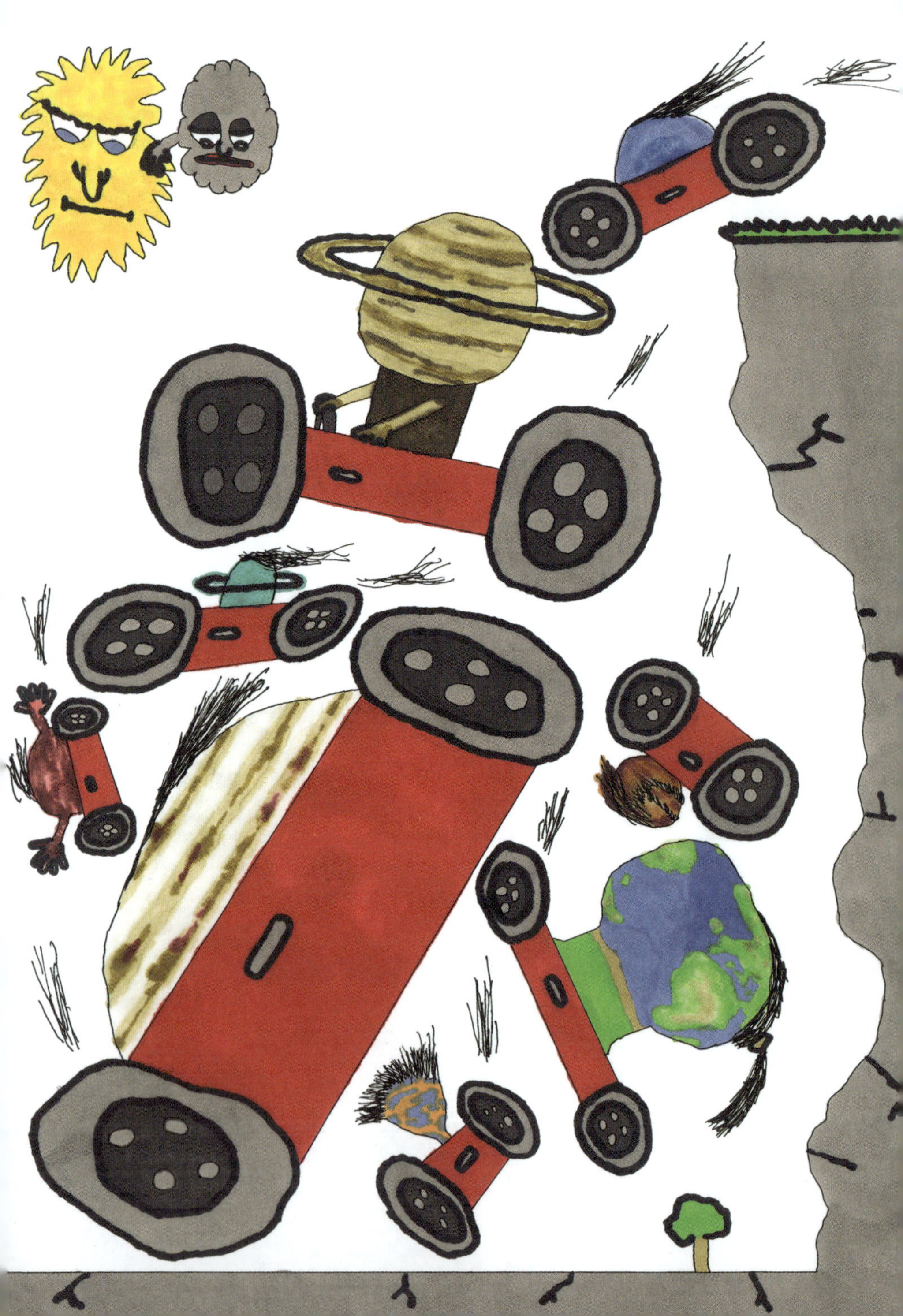

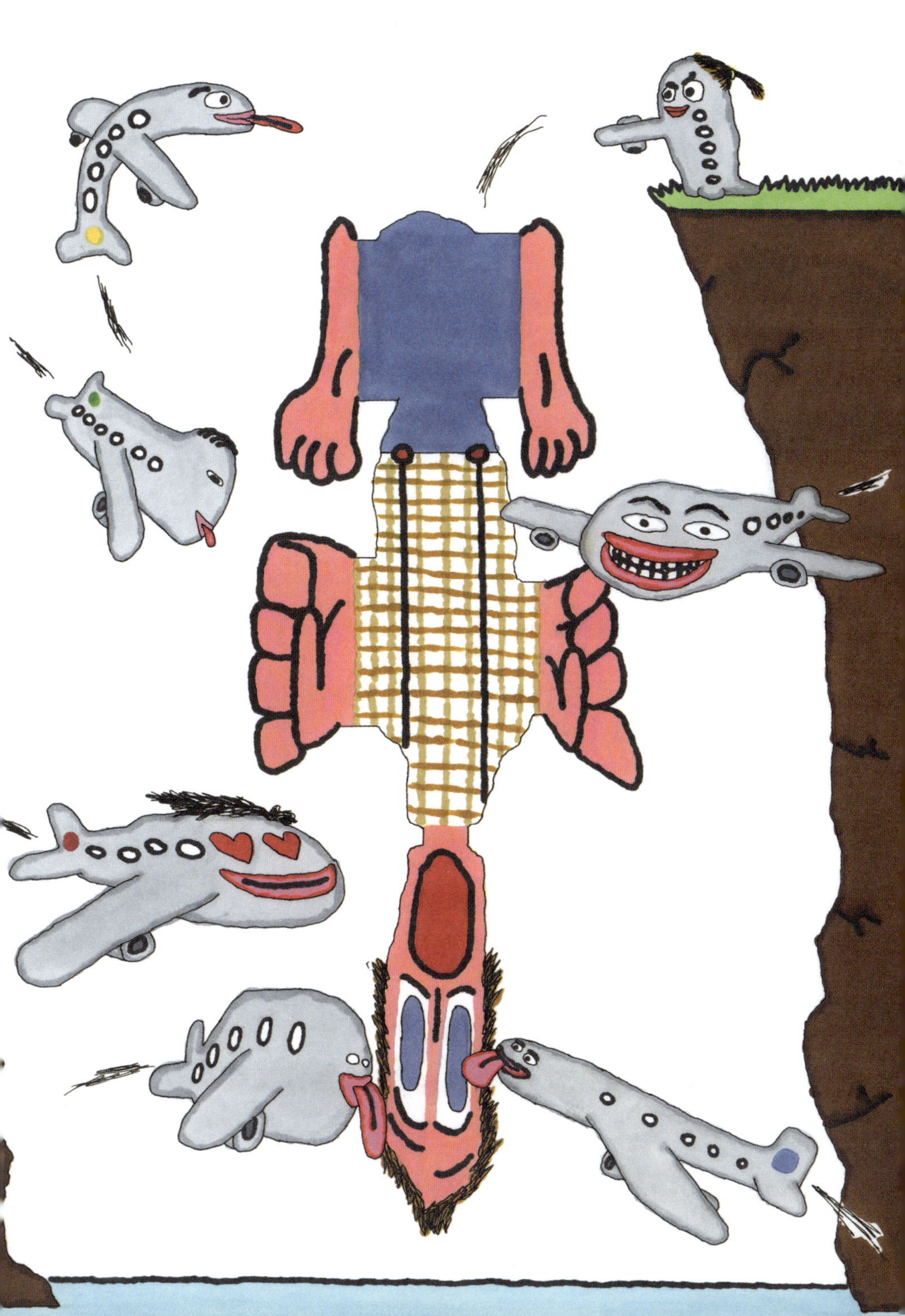

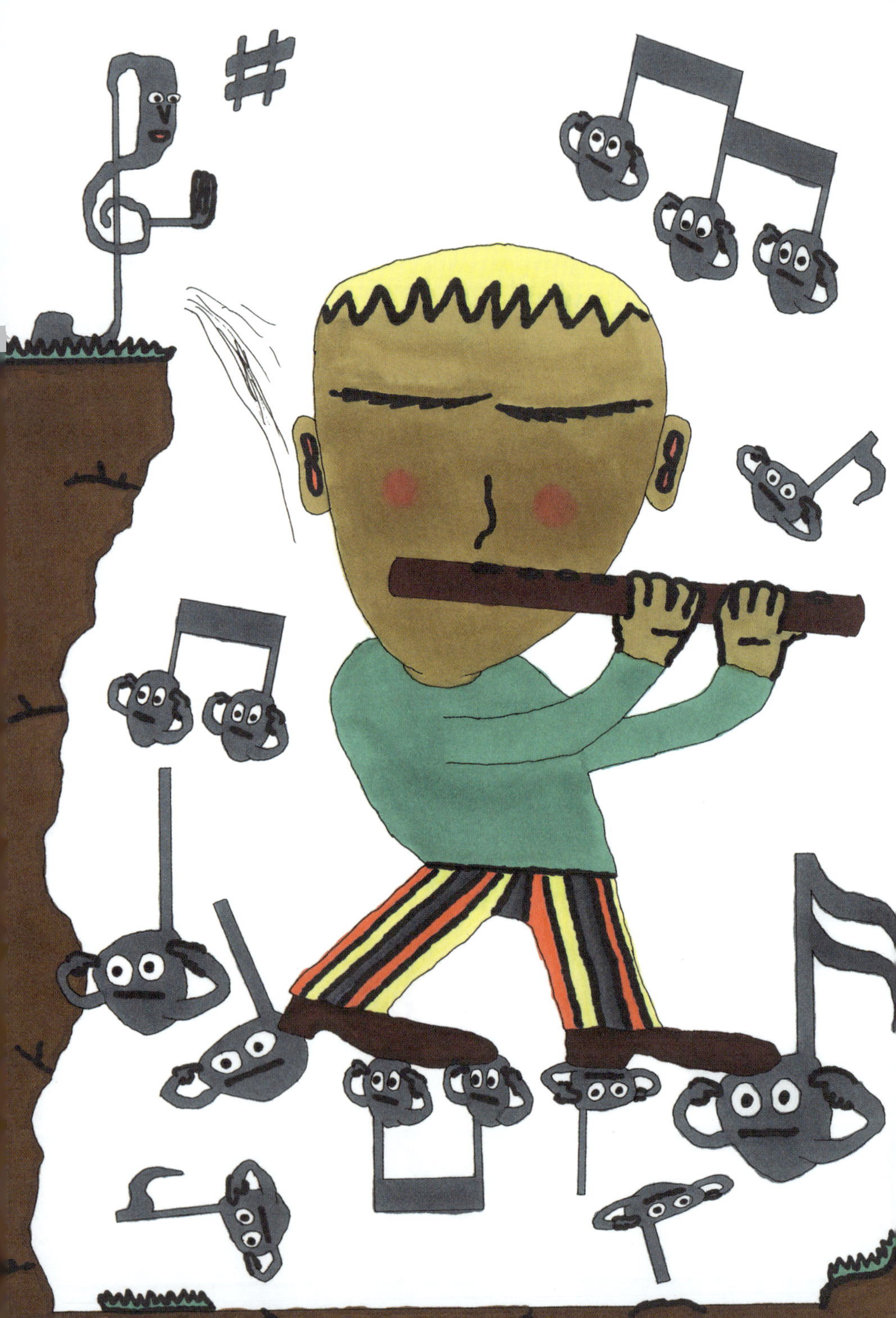

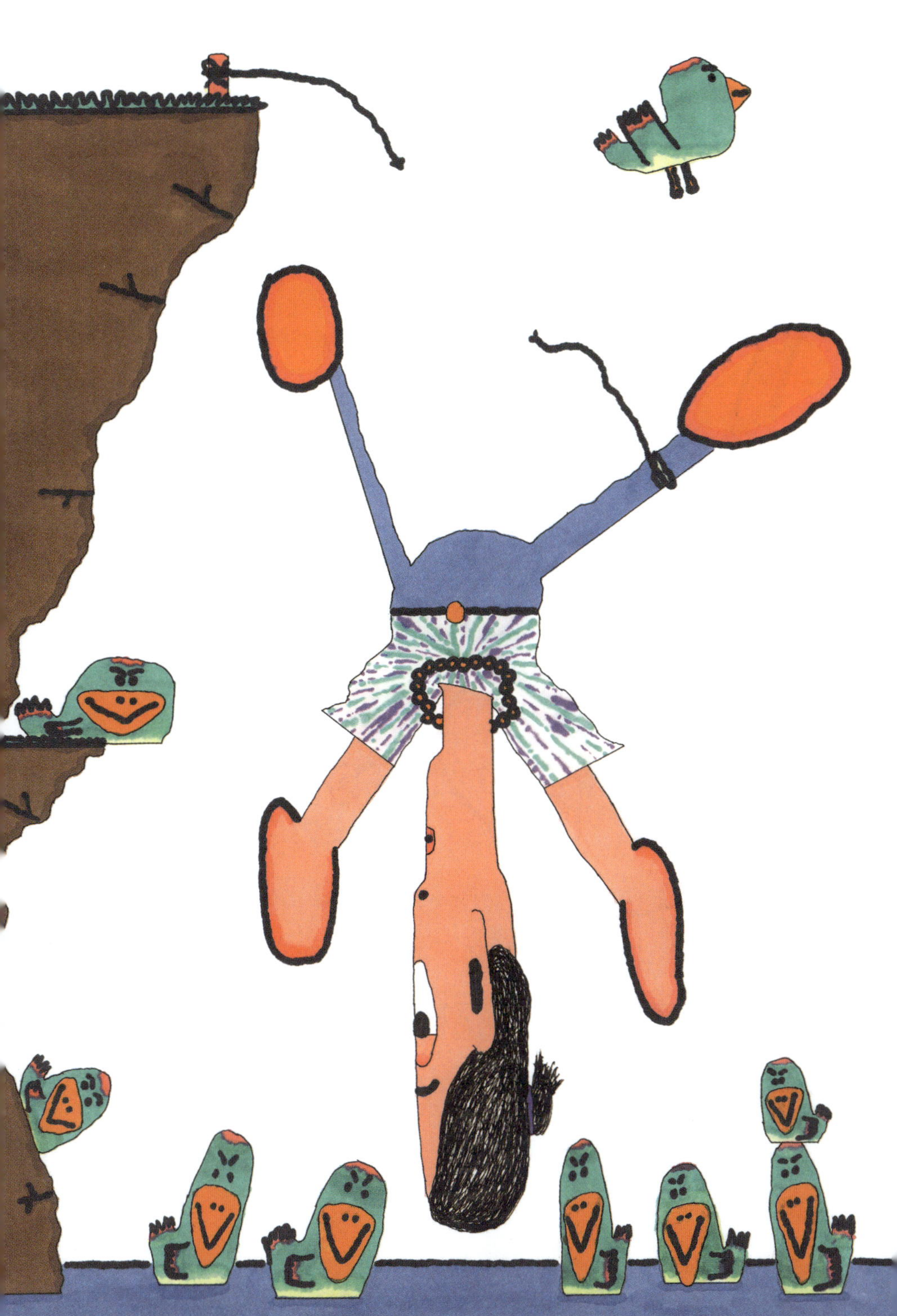

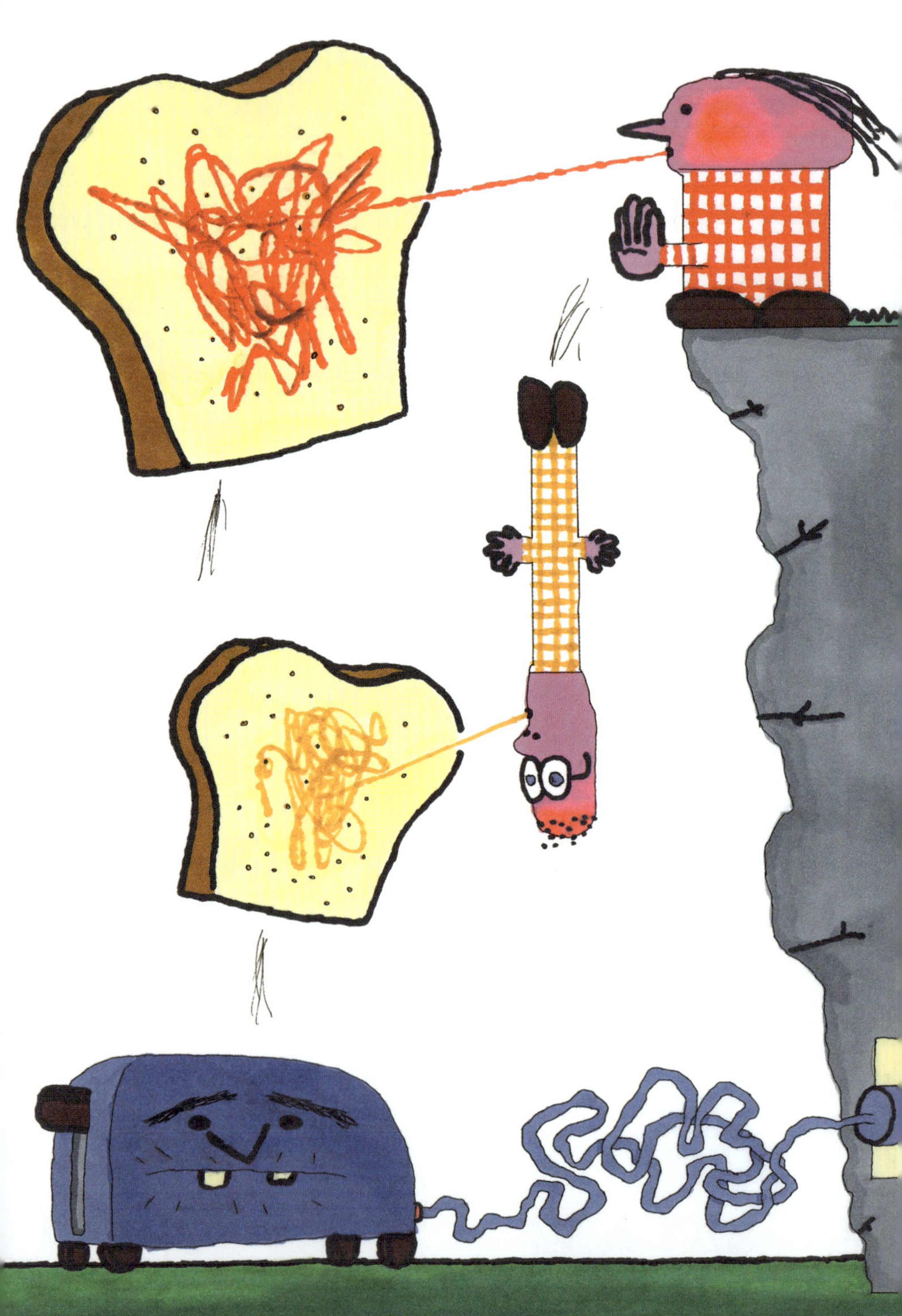

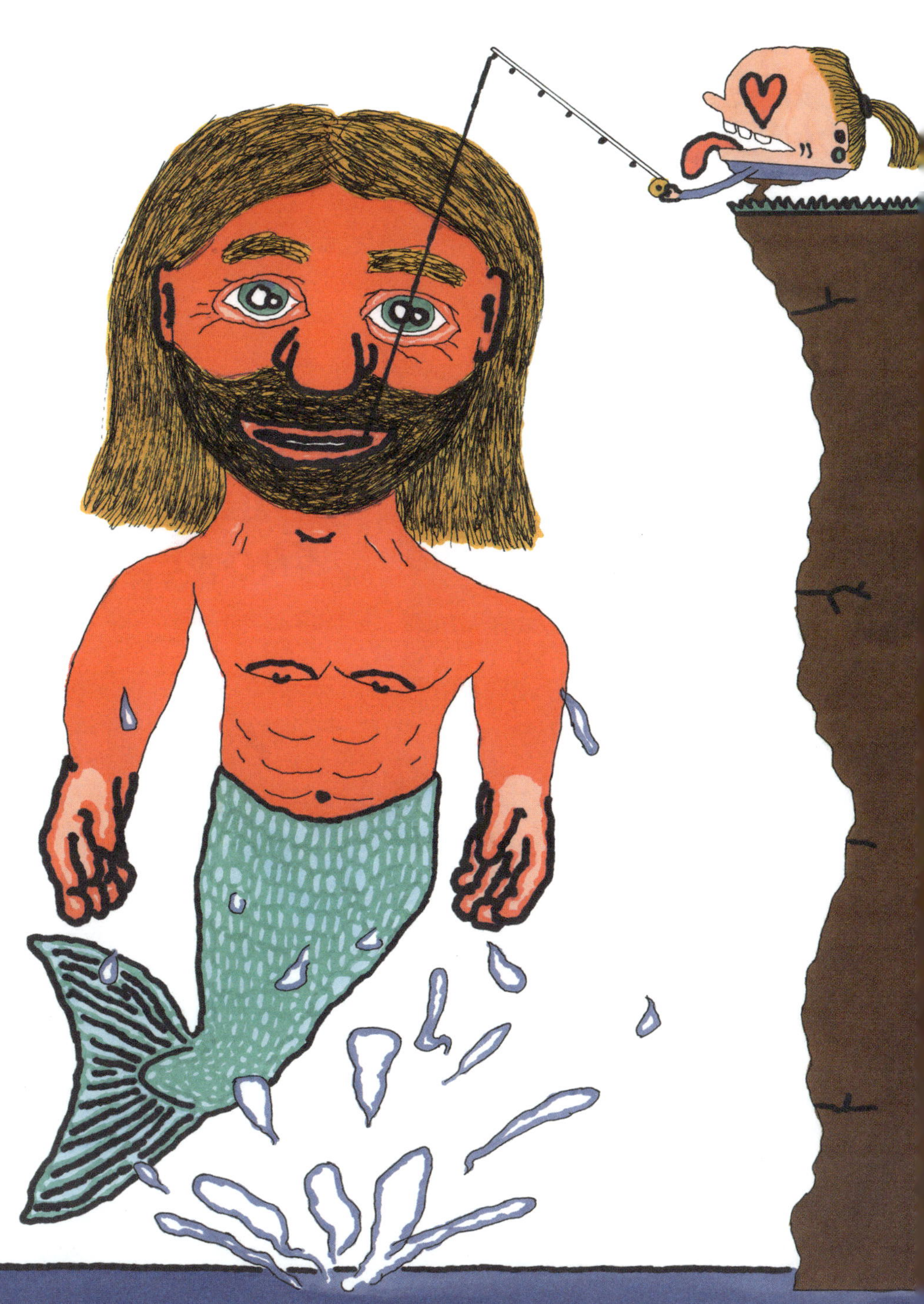

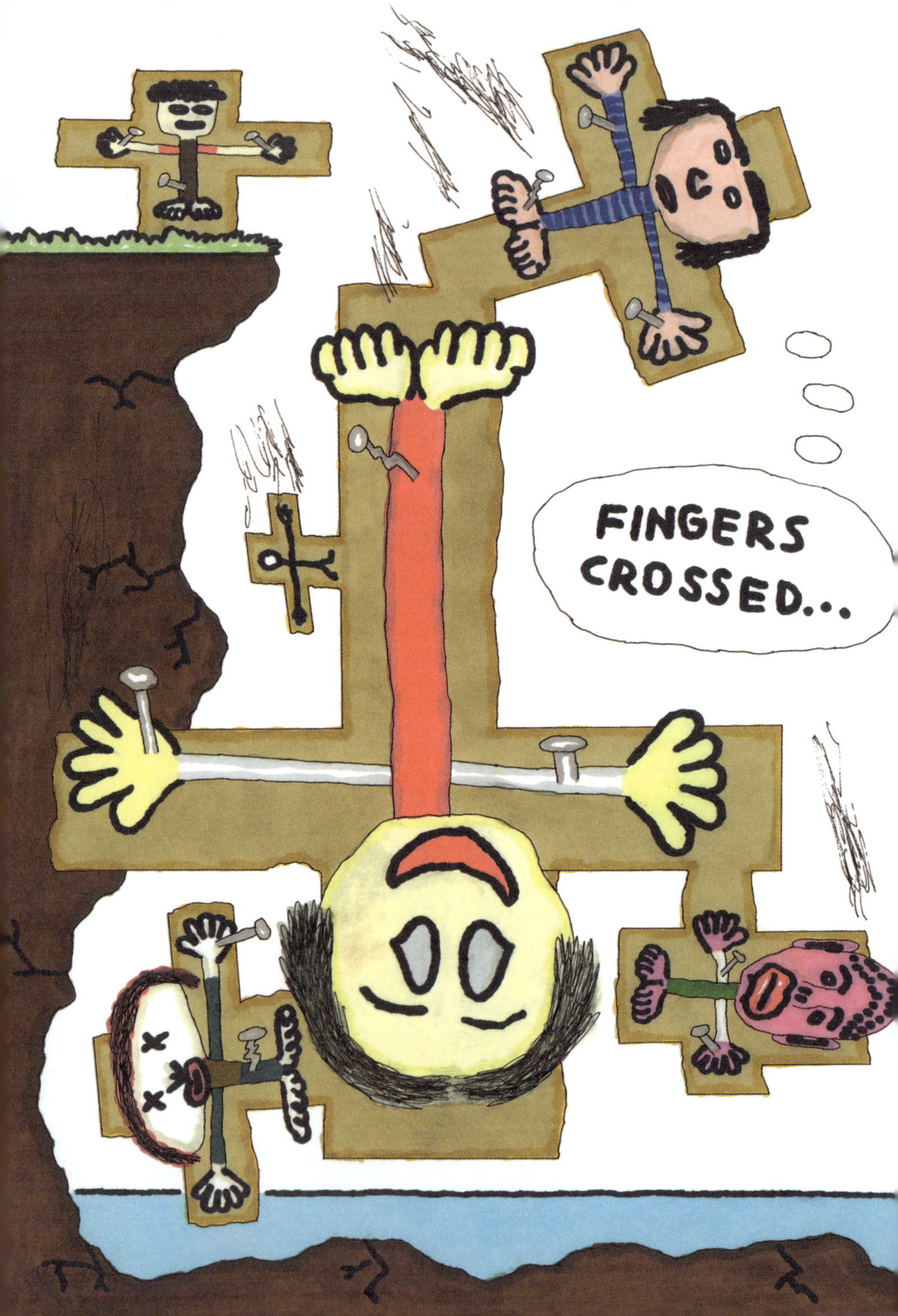
FINGERS CROSSED...

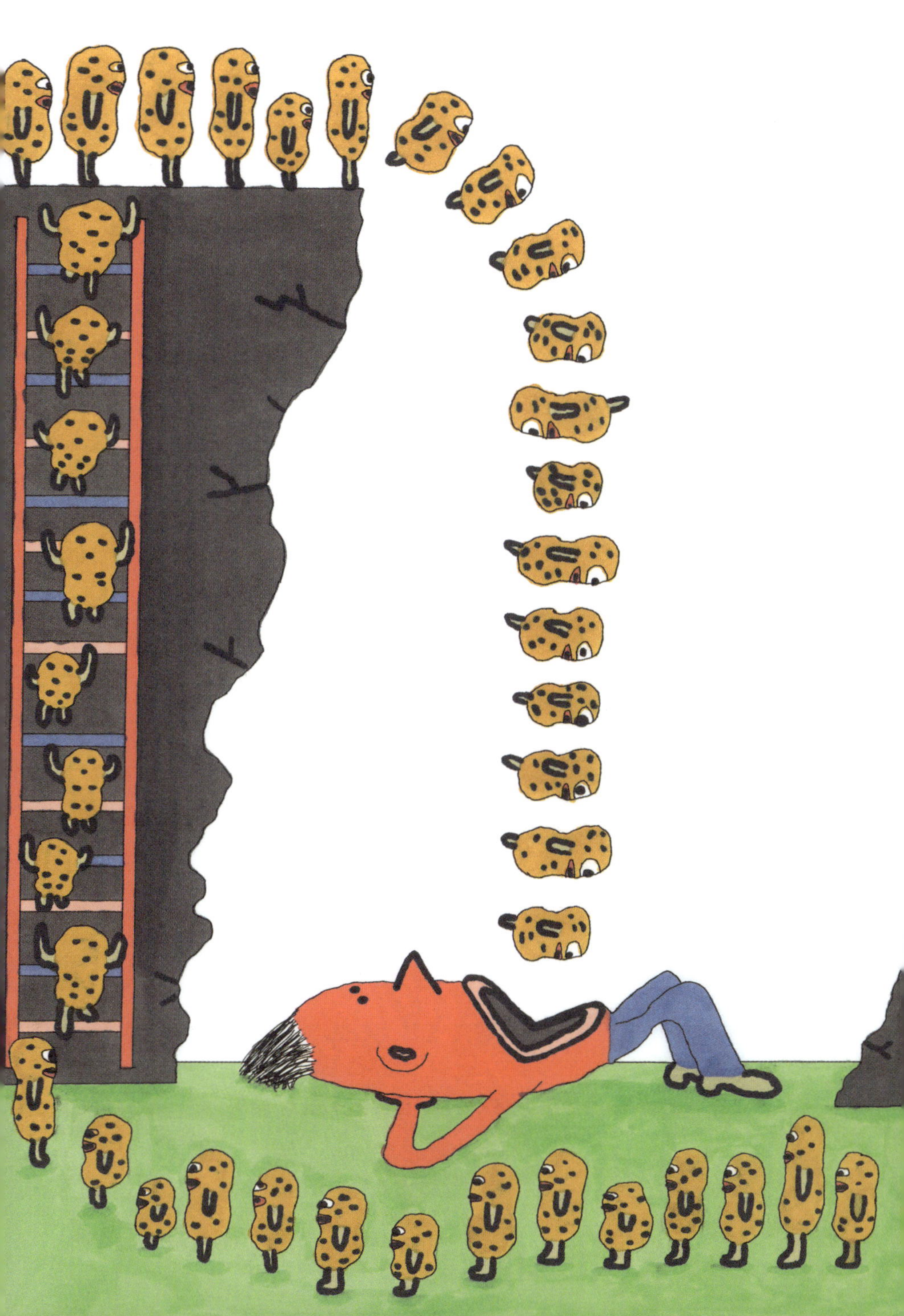

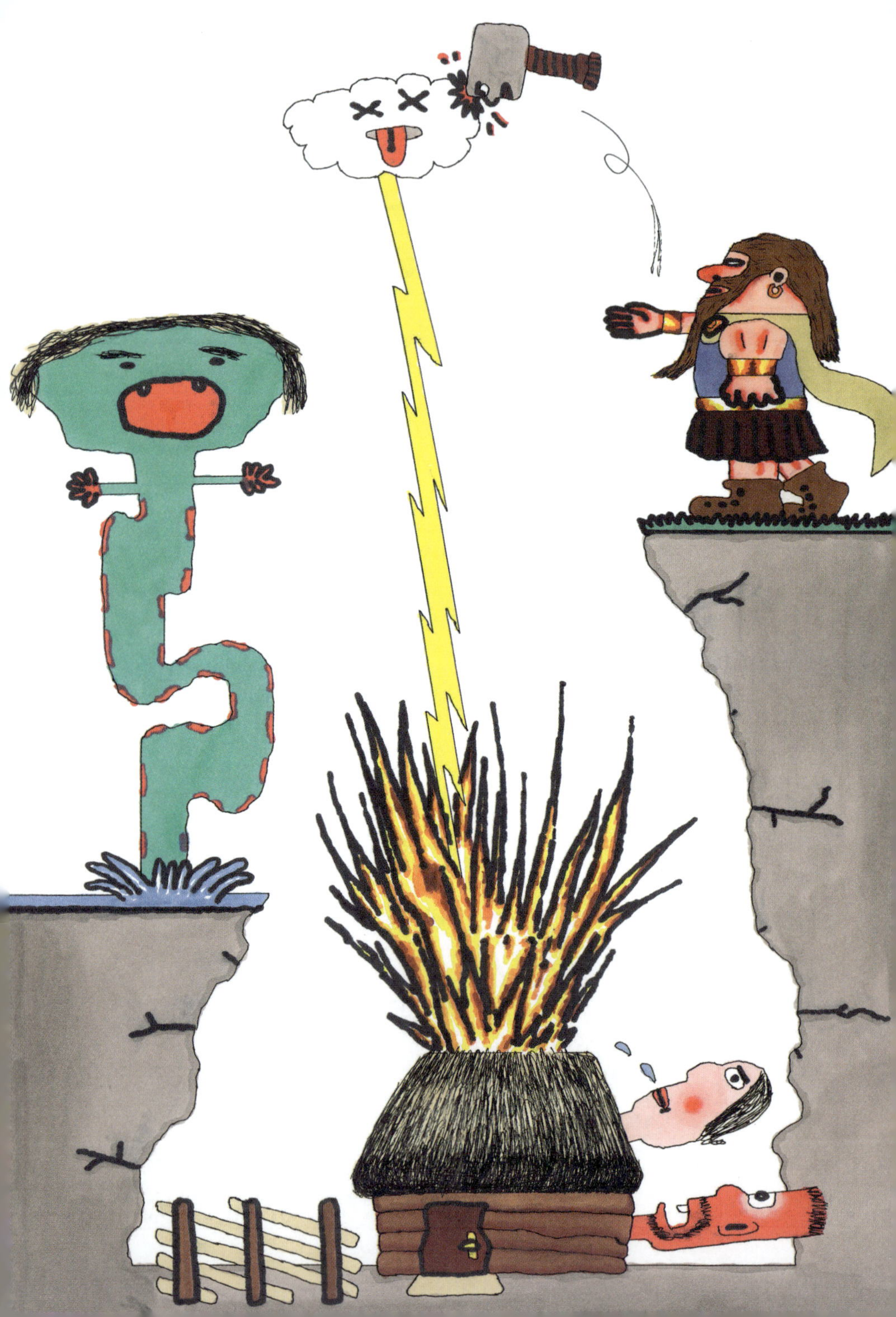

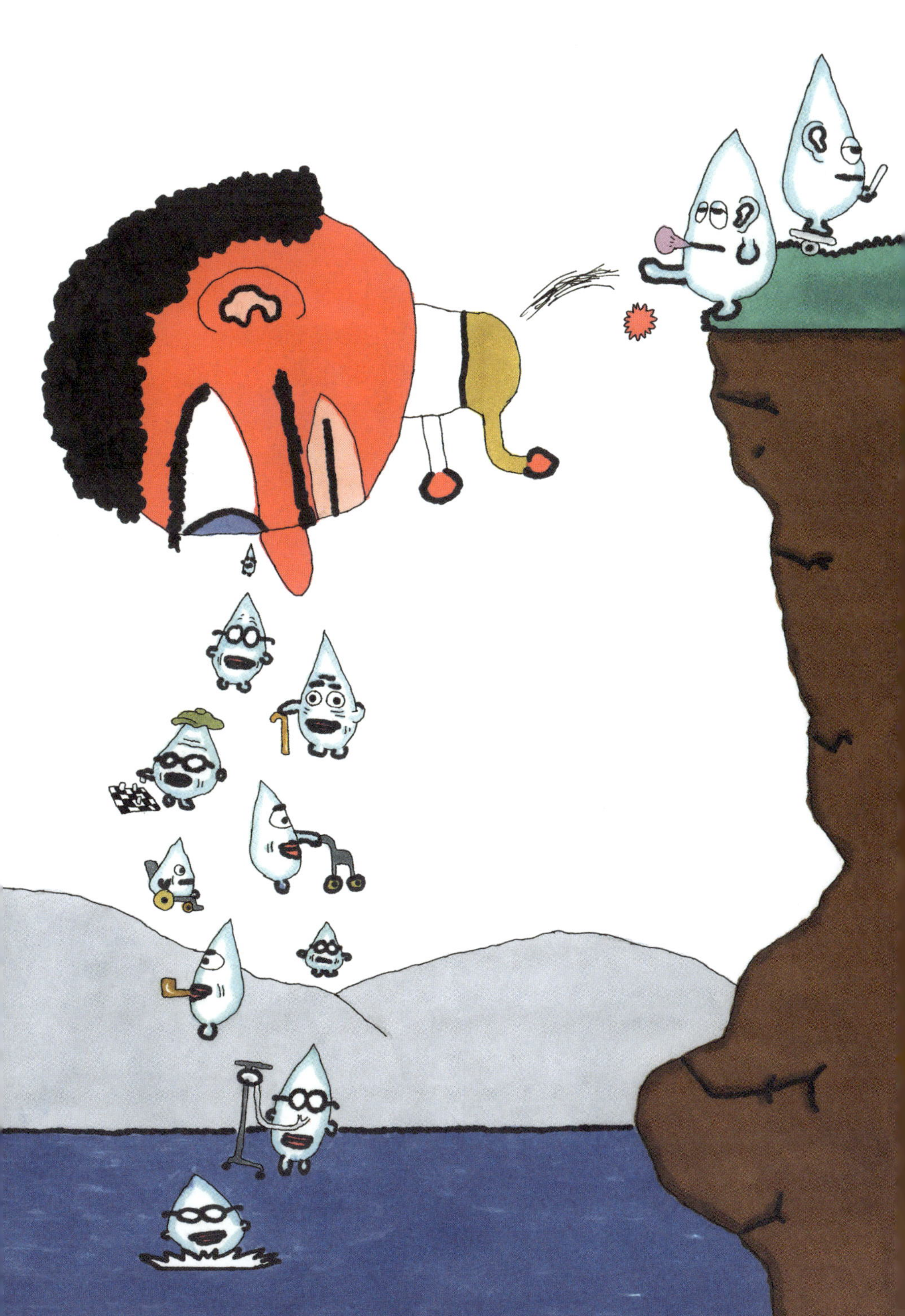

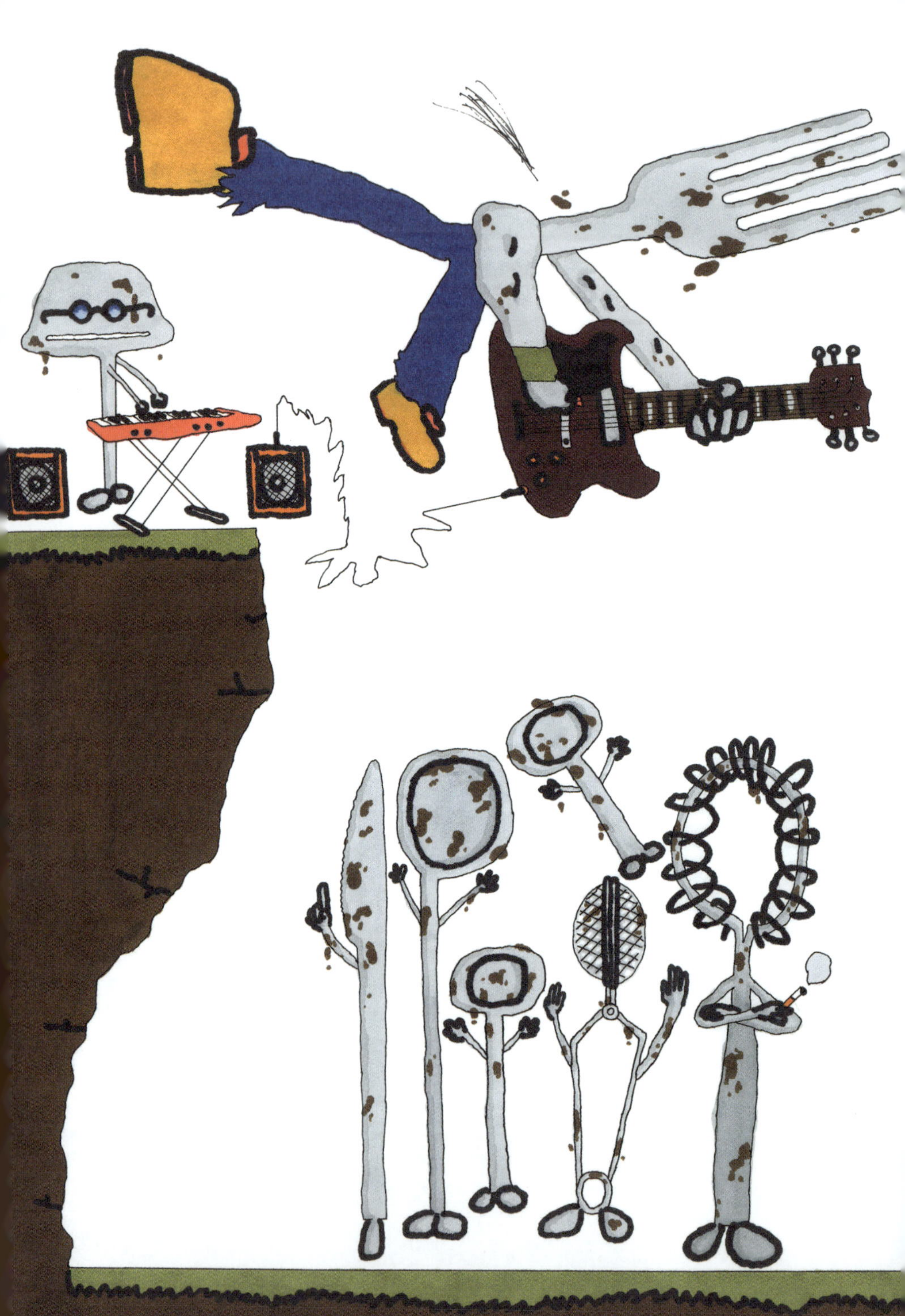

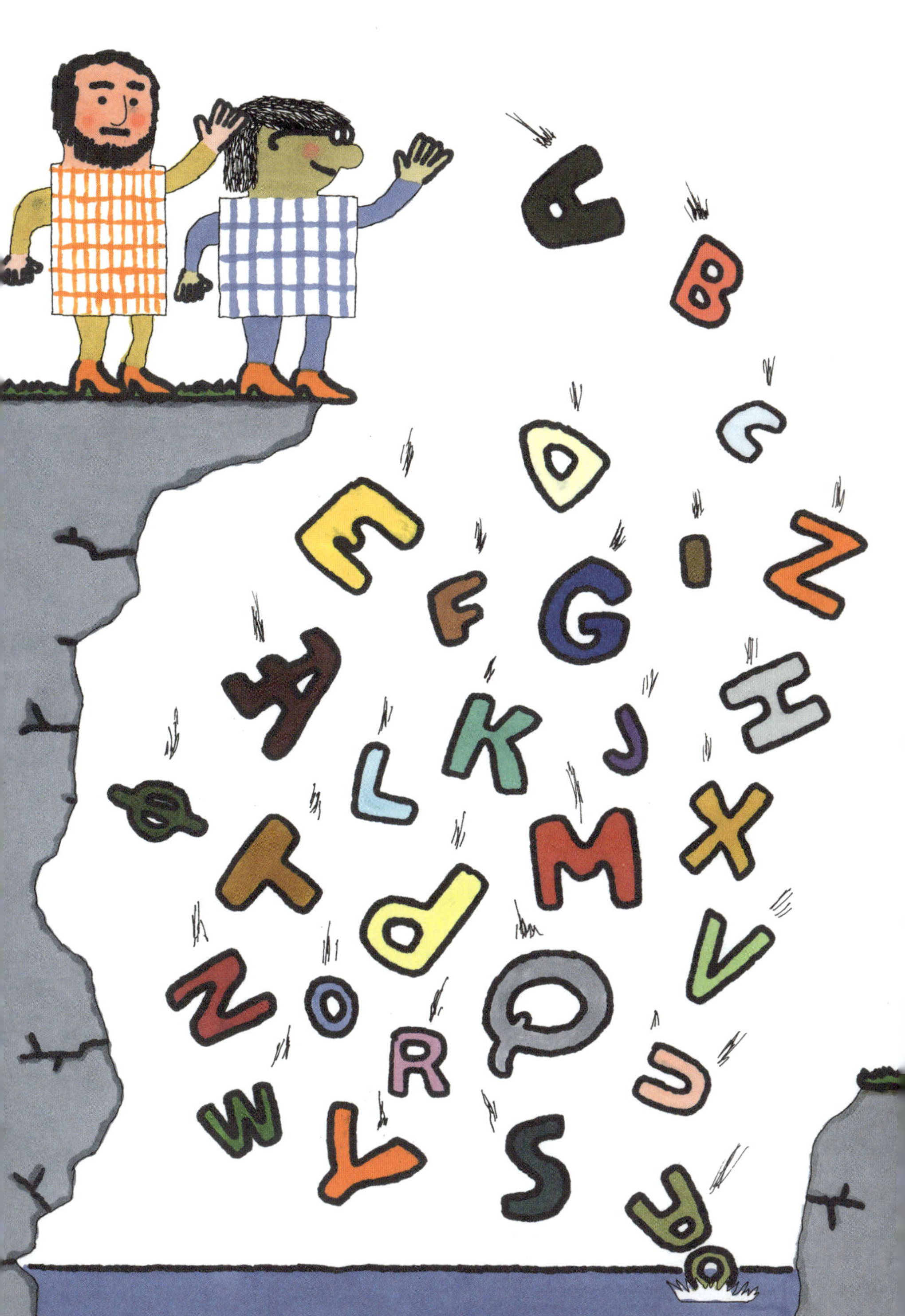

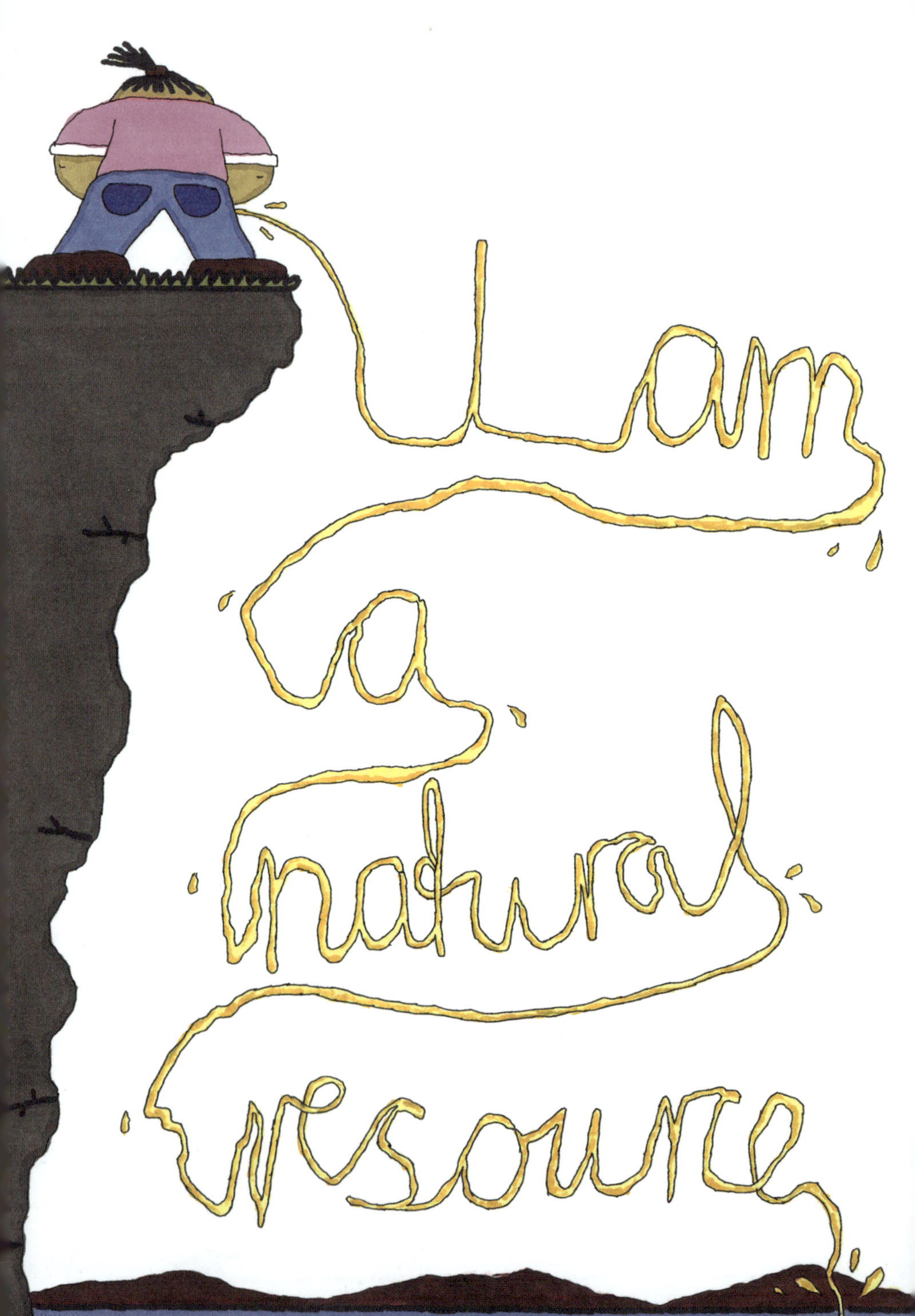
I am
a
natural
resource

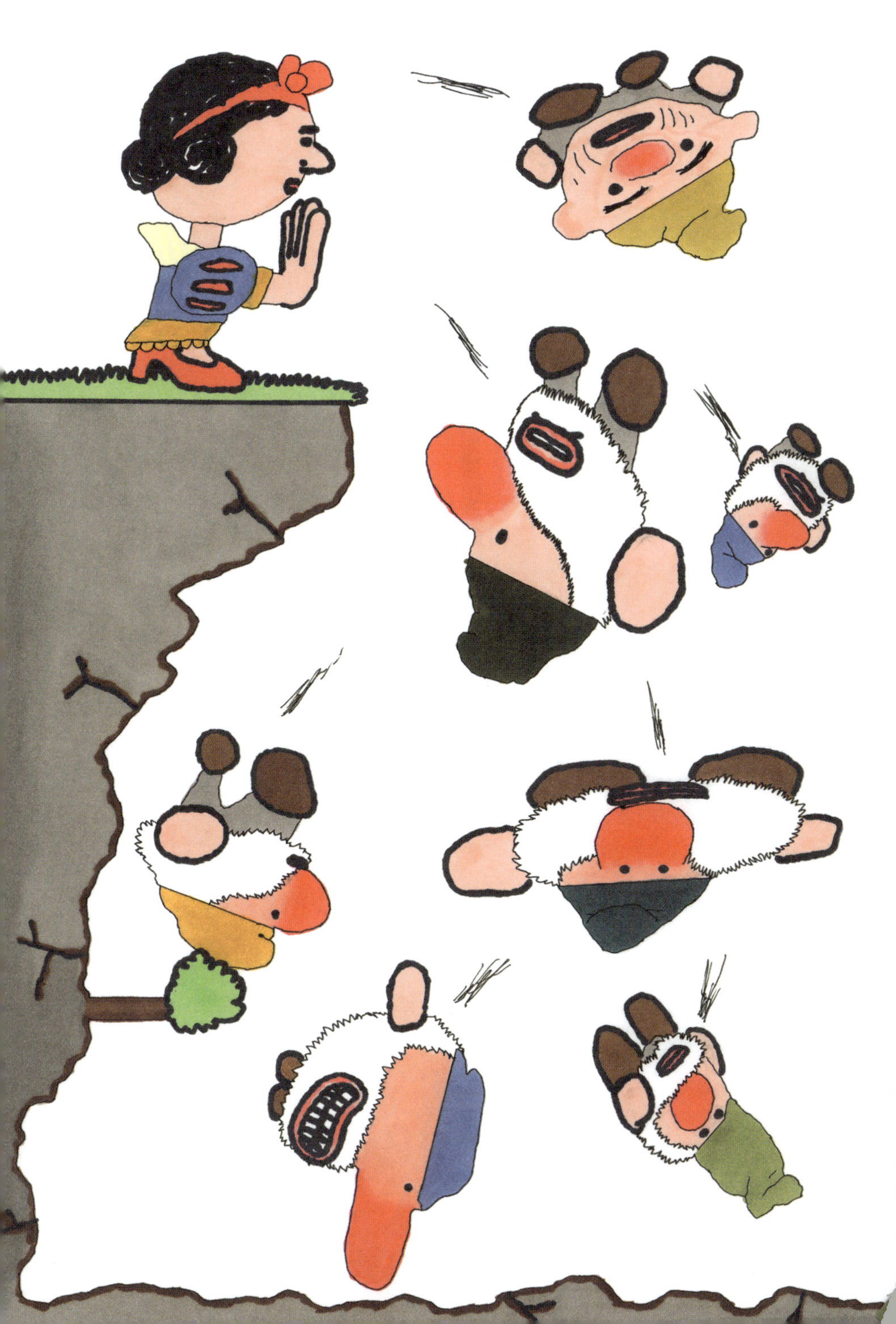

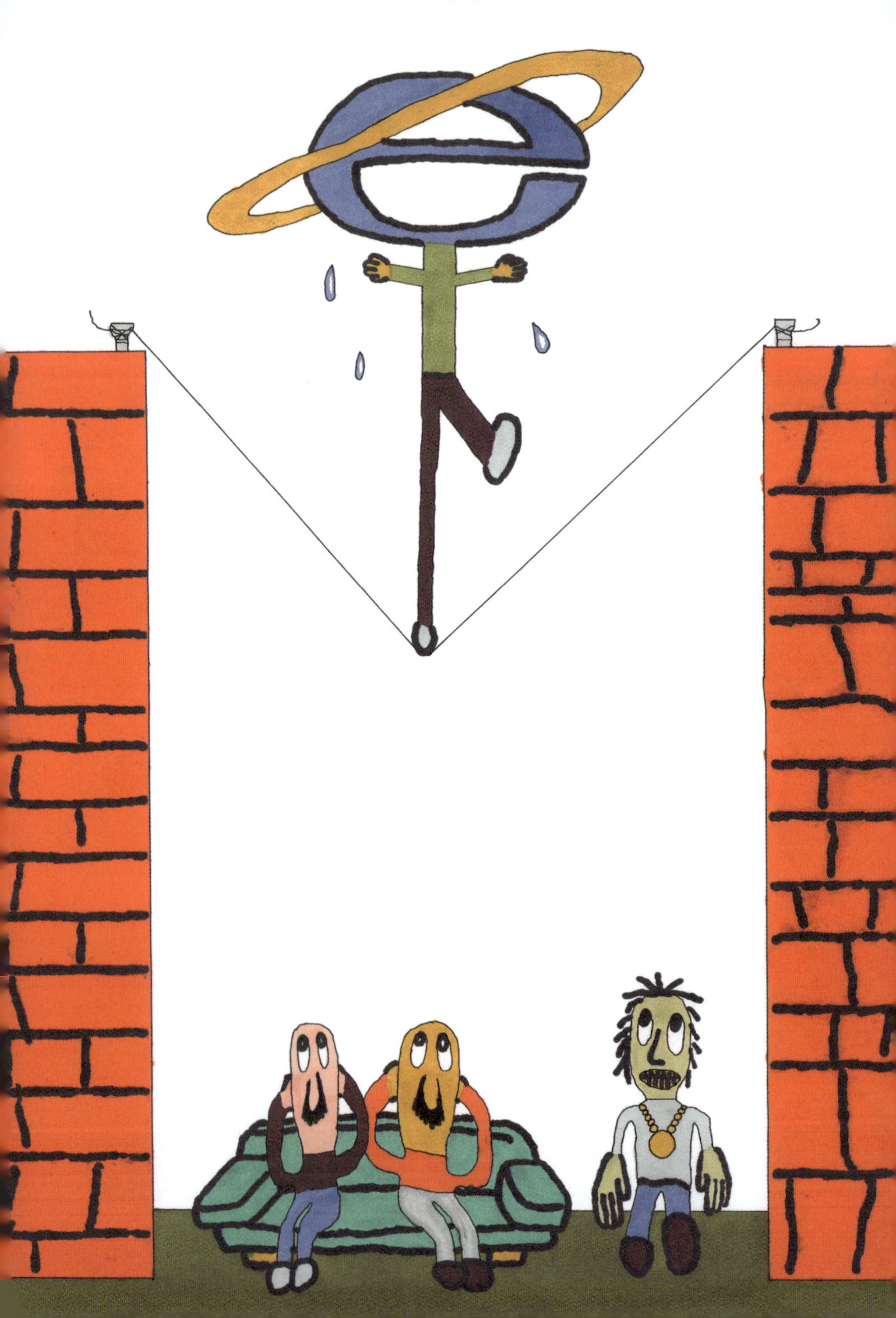

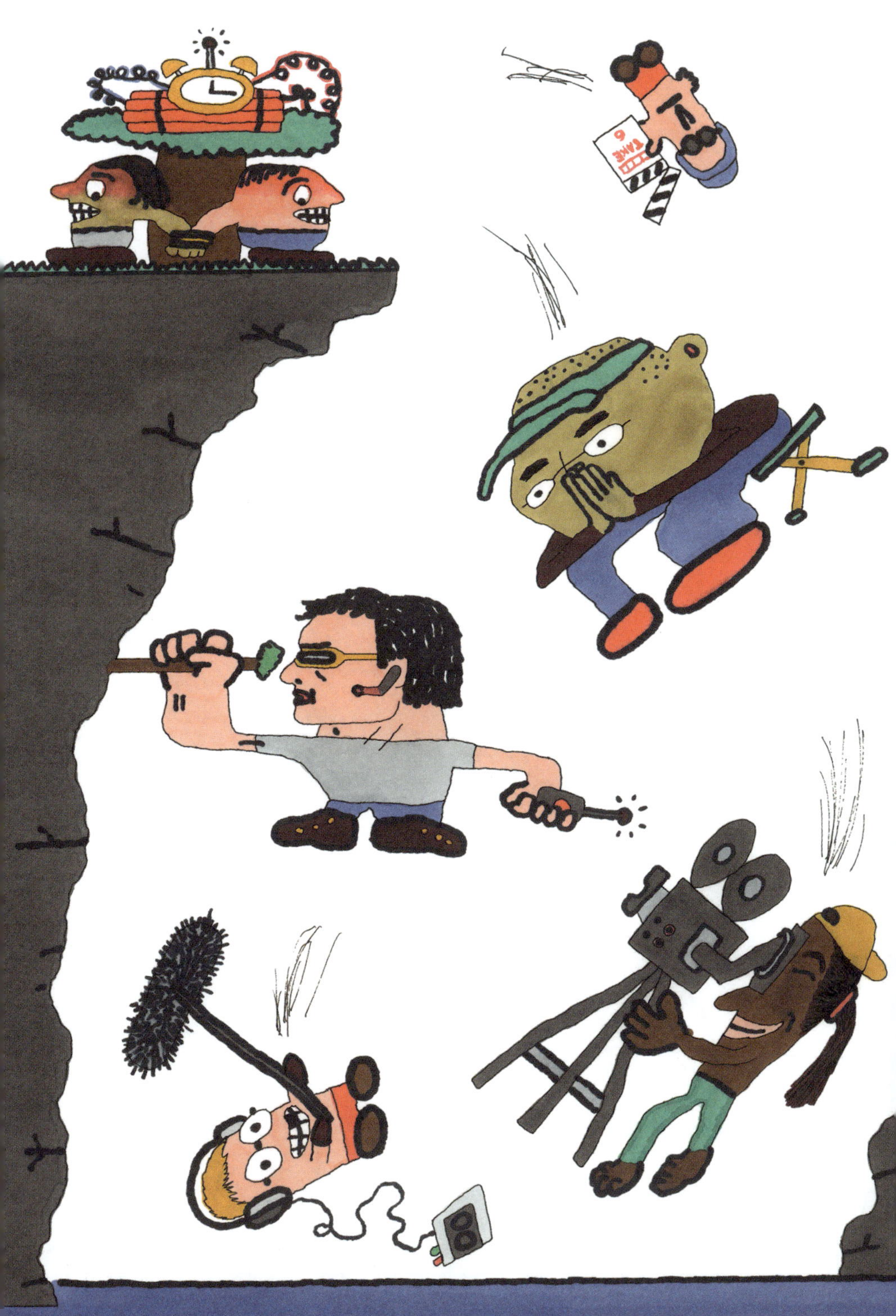
TAKE 6

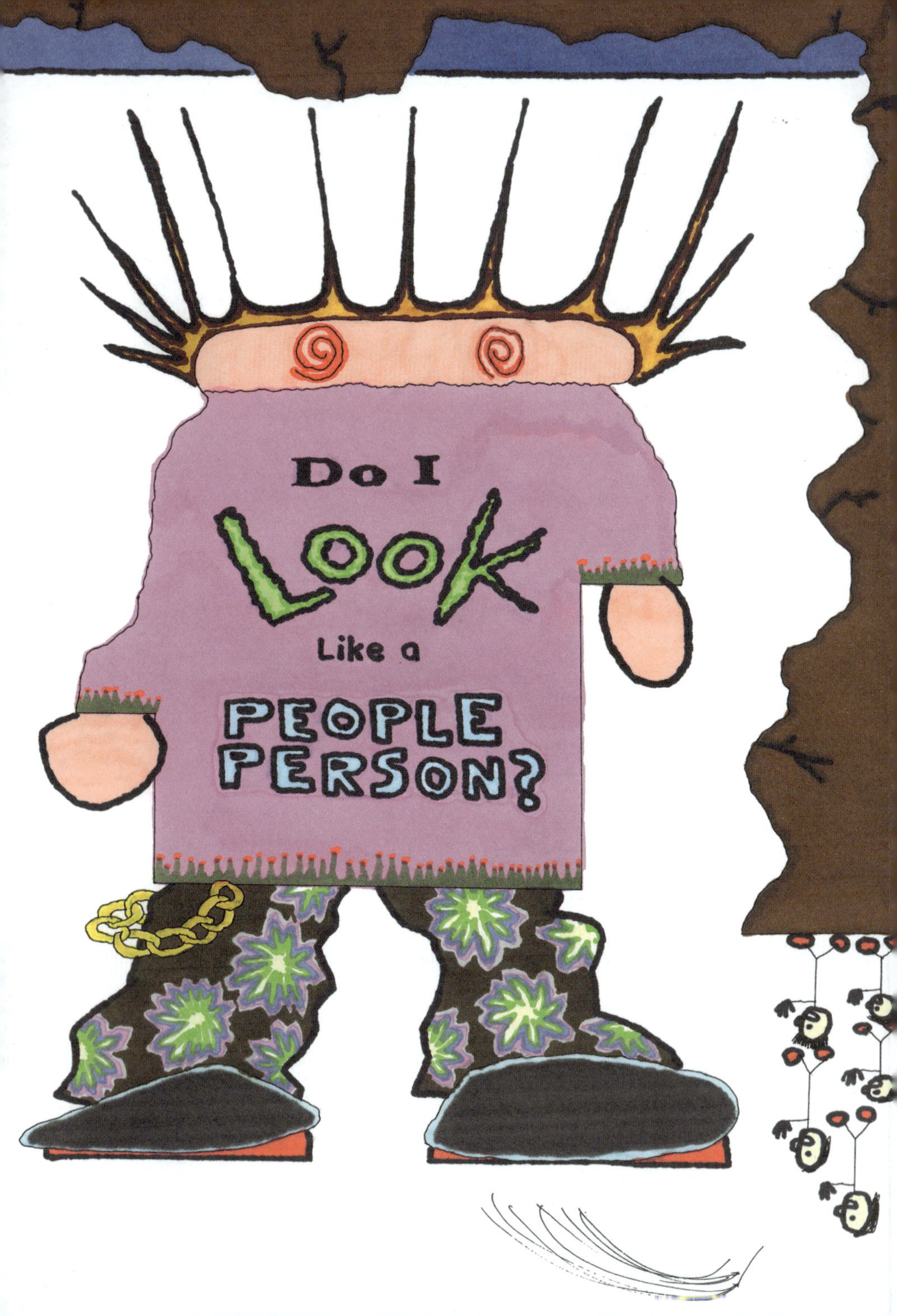
Do I
LOOK
Like a
PEOPLE
PERSON?

Fiscal Cliff
Erlend Peder Kvam

First Edition

Supported by Grafill
Published by Nieves
www.nieves.ch

ISBN 978-3-907179-29-1

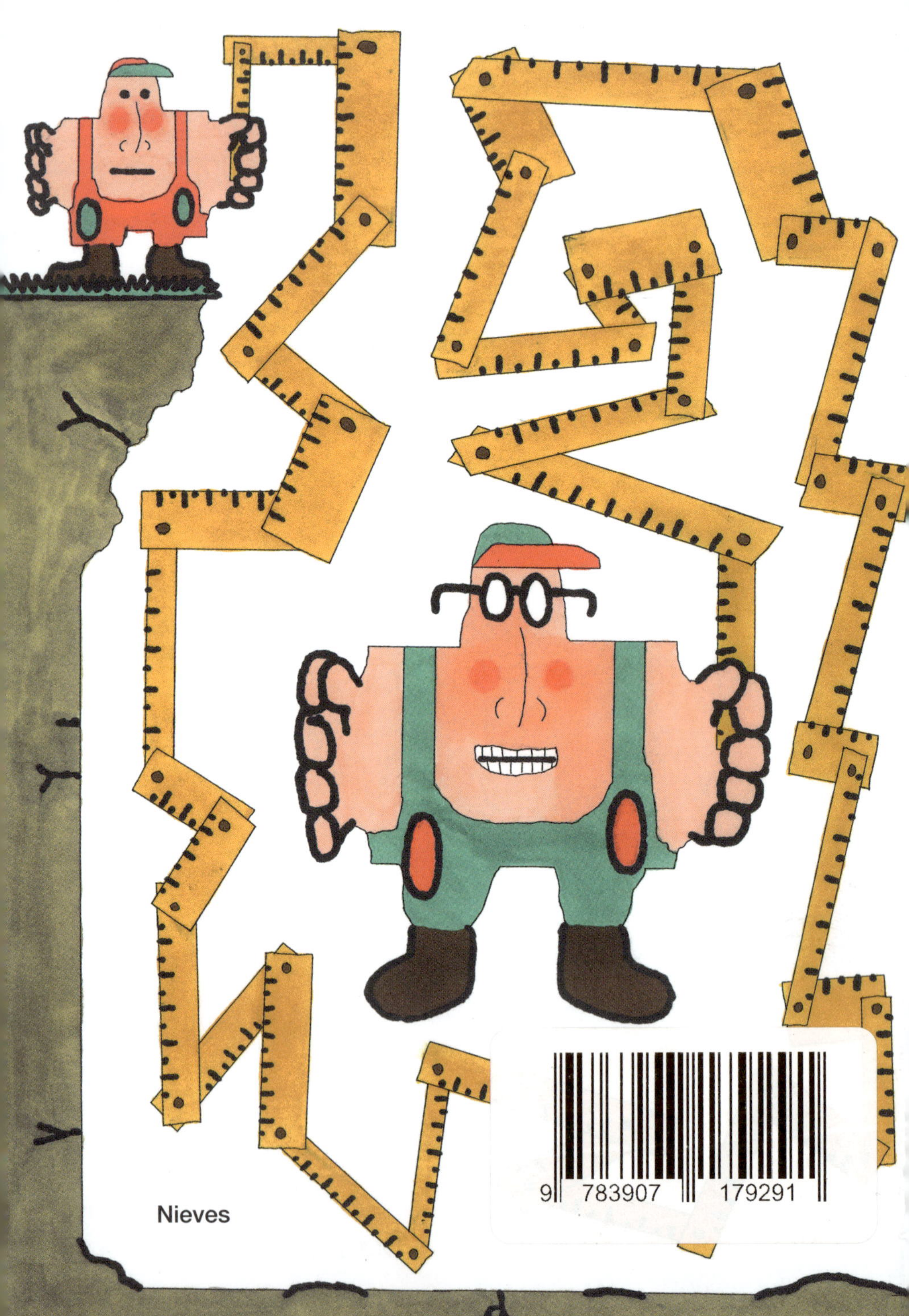
Nieves
9 783907 179291